ISLE OF WIGHT
CENTURY

1900–1999

Following page
1. Colliers often came into Cowes Harbour to unload at the two gas works or at the railway quay further up the river. Here, using baskets, a spritsail barge is being unloaded at a quay next to the Trinity House Wharf, East Cowes.

ISLE OF WIGHT
CENTURY
1900–1999

ROY BRINTON

THE DOVECOTE PRESS

2. On 29 December 1908 Hampshire and the Island were covered by a
blanket of snow which in some places was seven inches deep.
This scene at Clatterford, Carisbrooke, taken next day,
shows how much had fallen.

First published in 1999 by The Dovecote Press Ltd
Stanbridge, Wimborne, Dorset BH21 4JD

ISBN 1 874336 67 9

© Roy Brinton 1999

Typeset in Sabon by The Typesetting Bureau
Wimborne, Dorset
Printed and bound by
The Baskerville Press Ltd, Salisbury, Wiltshire

1 3 5 7 9 8 6 4 2

Contents

Introduction

At the beginning of the century the Isle of Wight had a population of about 82,000, with the main occupations being agriculture and manufacturing. Tourism was also increasingly important, as Queen Victoria's choice of a holiday home at Osborne had helped to make the Island a popular holiday destination. Raw materials had to be brought in by sea, so manufacturing industry was mainly concentrated around the mouth of the River Medina, where the shipbuilders J.S. White were the largest employers.

Stage coaches had been largely replaced by a railway network operated by three companies, the most profitable being the Ryde to Ventnor route, which carried the bulk of the tourist traffic. Life went on much as usual during the 1st World War, although, of course, many men were away in the armed forces.

The 1920s and '30s saw several changes in the life and economy of the Island. In the years following the 1st World War the recession hit the shipbuilders very hard, throwing many men out of work. The situation did not really improve until the late 1930s, but an industry which did grow was that of aviation, with aeroplanes being built by Samuel Saunders. Although farm tractors had started to appear after 1918, it was some years before they replaced the horse. With improvements in transport and more workers being allowed holidays, some paid, tourism continued to grow. The 1930s saw several concert halls and swimming pools being built. These, together with the rapid growth of the cinema, were also enjoyed by residents.

Like much of the British Isles, the Island was more affected by the 2nd World War. Right from the outbreak there were anti-aircraft batteries and radar stations. After France was occupied, more troops were posted to the Island to counter any threat of invasion. Towns and villages were bombed, 214 persons were killed and 552 houses were destroyed. Because of the mild climate Islanders were able to eke out their rations by growing fruit and vegetables. In the build up to D-Day in 1944 the Island filled with servicemen. Finally on the 5th November 1944 the air raid sirens sounded for the last time, as the war drew to a close.

Like the rest of Britain, the Island took a long time to recover. At first prefabricated bungalows arrived in 1946 to replace the houses destroyed and to provide homes for returning servicemen and their families. Then the local authorities gradually got underway with building housing estates. One of the first changes that Islanders saw after V.E. Day was the arrival of the holiday makers. During the next 20 years tourism continued to grow, with many families coming by train and boat to enjoy a fortnight beside the sea. This has now changed. Many of today's tourists arrive with their car at any time of the year, to enjoy a short break.

Changes came in the manufacturing industry with the closure of the shipbuilders J.S. White, and the arrival of the radar and electronics firm, Plessey. Intensified and highly mechanised agriculture has also brought changes. From being a main employer it now only employs about two per cent of the Island workforce. Today the Isle of Wight is a unitary authority and, with other public sectors, is the largest employer.

The greatest money earner is tourism which employs about a quarter of the workforce. Improvements to cross-Solent travel have helped to bring about two further changes. Because the mainland can now be reached in about ten minutes, a steady stream of workers commute as far as London. The second change is the increase in retired people who come to enjoy the climate, and now account for over a quarter of the Island's 130,000 residents.

ROY BRINTON, *August 1999*

3. As austerity gradually receded, people were able to travel more and coaches were built to meet this demand. Many holiday makers enjoyed the afternoon tours along the Military Road and rural West Wight, stopping at the Brighstone Tea Gardens for a cream tea.

Acknowledgements

I am very grateful to all those who have given of their knowledge and time to help make this book possible. They include the following: Chris Alldred, Norman Graham, John Hannam, Jack Lavers, Lord Mottistone, Ian Murray, Richard Newman, Society of the Propagation of the Gospel, Adrian Searle, Bill Shepard, Roger Silsbury and Ray Wheeler. My thanks are also due to my wife for checking the text.

I would also like to thank the following for allowing the inclusion of photographs in their possession or for which they hold the copyright: C Bancroft: 67; Ron Benton: 123; Britten-Norman: 103; Reg Davies: 65, 101; Debenhams, photographers: 96; A. Gale: 76; Hovertravel: 102; Isle of Wight Council: 133, 136, 139, 140; Isle of Wight Railway: 61, 66, 110; Ian Murray: 118; W. J. Nigh & Sons Ltd: 122; Norman Paterson: 82; Roger Smith: 117; The late Frank Taylor: 87, 97, 111, 113, 126, 132, 134; Joy Warren: 120; Derek Warman: 6; G.K.N. Westland: 85, 93, 109; S. Woodnutt: 119.

1900-1909 New Century, New Ideas

4. The death of Queen Victoria brought to an end a great period in the Island's history. The Queen died at Osborne on 22 January 1901, having reigned for 63 years 7 months. On the morning of 1 February the funeral procession started from Osborne House, and is seen here at Trinity Pier, East Cowes, preparing to embark on the Royal Yacht *Alberta*.

5. Signor Guglielmo Marconi had been carrying out wireless experiments at the Needles since December 1897, but in May 1900 he decided to move. He called on Mr. Kirkpatrick of Windcliffe, Niton, to request permission to set up a station at Knowles Farm, near St. Catherine's lighthouse. Later that year Mr. Kirkpatrick's daughter received a message from her future brother-in-law on board *H.M.S. Vernon*, one of the first private wireless messages to be received anywhere in the world.

6. Sandown Grammar School was first opened in 1901 as a Higher Grade Elementary School for 150 pupils. With the passing of the Education Act of 1902, the school became the first secondary school on the Island. In 1960 the school moved to a new site on the edge of Sandown.

7. At the beginning of the century Newport Borough needed to increase the area to which it supplied water, employing a Southampton contractor to construct a reservoir on the down above Carisbrooke. When finished, the reservoir held 800,000 gallons, and was brought into use in May 1902.

8. In August 1903 Princess Beatrice unveiled a memorial to her mother Queen Victoria in St. James's Square, Newport. The figures at the base are Dignity, Fortitude and Sympathy upholding the crown, and the whole memorial was designed by local architect Percy Stone.

9. The foundation stones of the Technical Institute and Free Library at Newport were laid on 23 July 1902, and the building was completed eighteen months later. In practise the building was used in the day time as a Pupil-Teacher Centre and in the evening for lectures. The Free Library occupied the right hand wing of the building.

10. Due to anti-clerical laws passed in France in 1901, a community of Benedictine monks came to reside at Appuldurcombe House. They only had a short lease and in 1907 purchased the Victorian-built Quarr Abbey House. Work on building a new abbey started straightaway and during the next year the monks started to move into the new buildings.

11. In April 1905 the first motor buses on the Island started to operate from Ryde Esplanade to the various towns. Unfortunately the roads could not withstand their weight and many buses became stuck in mud. There was also a lack of passengers at the end of the season, so the buses were withdrawn.

12. (*Following pages*) Harry Margham and his wife proudly showing milk floats and wagons built in his own workshops, at an agricultural show. Harry came to the Island in 1884 and a few years later started his own business in Crocker Street, Newport.

13. Ryde's lifeboat *Selina* was called out on New Year's Day 1907, and, after about three hours of searching for a man reported to be adrift in an open boat, was capsized by a sudden gust of wind. Two of the crew died of exhaustion. Their funeral service was held at St. James's Church and this photograph shows the carriages which followed the hearse along Lind Street.

14. *H.M.S. Gladiator* capsized after being in collision with the American liner *St. Paul* on the 25 April 1908. The weather was bad and as the up-turned cruiser drifted towards Sconce Point, west of Yarmouth, she rolled onto her starboard side throwing many sailors into the sea. Twenty-nine men died, most of them drowned.

15. The Isle of Wight Volunteers were formed in 1859, and, after the Territorial Army Act of 1907, became Princess Beatrice's Isle of Wight Rifles. Summer camps were very popular with the men as they received normal pay, plus an annual bounty of £5.

16. Albany Barracks was established at Parkhurst in 1798, but was partially rebuilt in 1895 and occupied about 100 acres. Various regiments used the barracks – this is the band of the 2nd Battalion of the Suffolk Regiment.

17. The Royal Needles Hotel (otherwise known as the Alum Bay Hotel) was destroyed by fire in 1909. The nineteenth century building had been very popular with visitors to the area. The owner William Berkeley had retired that year and it was rumoured that the building had been set alight to make an insurance claim.

18. This steam bus belonged to Creeths of Nettlestone and was purchased, second-hand, in 1909. It had been built in 1907 and was originally used in Scotland. In this photograph the bus had been hired by the St. Helens' Band of Hope for an outing in 1912. Creeths operated steam buses until 1923, being the last firm to do so.

19. Three sovereigns – King Edward VII flanked left by the Prince of Wales, later King George V and right by Prince Edward, later King Edward VIII. They were photographed aboard the Royal yacht *Victoria & Albert*.

1910-1919 Peace and War

20. In her will Queen Victoria left Osborne Cottage, East Cowes, to her youngest daughter, Princess Beatrice (standing fourth from the left), where this photograph was taken in 1910. Princess Beatrice's daughter Queen Victoria Eugenie is seated to the left, and to the right is her husband King Alfonso of Spain.

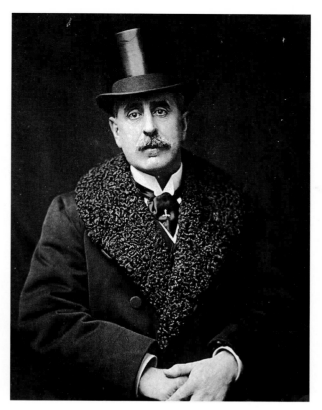

21. Seated here is Major-General J.E.B. Seely (later 1st Lord Mottistone) who served in both the Boer and 1st World Wars. He was born in 1868, the son of Sir Charles Seely of Brook House. General Seely was elected M.P. for the Island in 1900, in his absence, whilst serving in South Africa.

22. In the December 1910 General Election the Island seat was won by 223 votes, by Douglas Hall, Conservative. His Liberal opponent was Constantine Scaramonga Ralli, born in London in 1854. He had been in the banking business for many years and later became an author. His home was West Hill House, Shanklin.

23. Outside Newchurch Post Office on Shrove Tuesday 1911. The sub-postmaster John Wheeler is about to carry out the local tradition of throwing sweets into the air, to be scrambled for by the children. The tradition finished in 1913.

24. (*Opposite page, top*) A few years after Marconi moved his wireless experiments to Niton the Marconi Company erected a Lloyds Signal and Wireless Telegraphy Station about half-a-mile away. In about 1910 it was taken over by the General Post Office.

25. (*Opposite page, bottom*) In August 1911 an aviation exhibition was arranged for Ventnor Week, but due to various mishaps several competitors were unable to get over from the mainland. One entry who did make it is seen here flying over Orchard Bay.

26. This is a scene which could be seen each summer on the Island's roads. The roads were maintained by spraying hot tar followed by spreading gravel, and finally this heavy Aveling steam roller consolidated the new surface. In 1912 the I.W. Rural District Council was concerned about the high cost of providing this type of surface.

27. Petty Officer John Humber died of lockjaw in March 1913, aged 38 years, as the result of a cycle accident on Mersley Down. His body was brought back to the Island from the mainland, landed at Ryde Pier, placed on the tram truck and taken to the Pier Gates for its final journey to West Street Cemetery.

28. This photograph was taken during the 1st World War at the rear of Hazelwood House, Ryde. The house had been used by the Y.M.C.A., but was taken over by the Government and used as a convalescent home for soldiers, under the supervision of the County Hospital. Here a patient can be seen imitating 'Kaiser Bill', the German Emperor William II.

29. During the 1st World War hundreds of soldiers were brought into the Ryde area to recover from their wounds. To meet their needs a War Supply Depot was opened: here local ladies can be seen preparing dressings and bandages for delivery to the three hospitals in the area.

30. Having read of the devastation caused in war time Belgium by the German Army two farmers decided in 1916 to tour the Island to collect donations of farm implements, produce and stock. These were sold on a Saturday in St. James's Square, Newport. The sale raised £700 which was sent to the King of the Belgiums to be used to repair and replace orchards.

31. One of the 150 German submarines that surfaced and surrendered when the 1st World War ended in November 1918 was brought to J.S. White's Thetis Yard, East Cowes, and opened for public inspection for four days in 1919. U123 had sunk Allied shipping off the coast of America.

32. After the 1st World War, a naval tower no longer needed by the Navy was given to Trinity House and towed on a calm day in 1920 from Shoreham, where it was built (right hand tower), to the entrance to Spithead. There it was settled in 12 fathoms of water to replace the Nab lightvessel. The tower stands 90 feet above the waves and was staffed by three men. Today it is automated.

33. This alas poor quality photograph is of one of the earliest tractors on the Island, and is shown working on Rowborough Farm, near Shorwell, in about 1919. It was built by Henry Garner Ltd., of Birmingham, had four cylinders and ran on paraffin.

34. In the days of the horse-drawn hay wagon everybody leant a hand getting in the hay crop and building a stack. Here, at Shate Farm, Brighstone, men and boys are helping, together with the lady who has brought the tea.

35. From the middle of the last century until the present day Seaview has been popular with visitors in search of a peaceful holiday in sight of the sea. Here a small yacht is crowded with well-dressed ladies and gentlemen enjoying a trip on the water in fine weather.

36. This family was typical of the growing number of holiday-makers that came to the Island in the 1920s. They were photographed on Sandown Pier during the local regatta. The pier was erected in 1878 and the Pavilion in the background was built in 1895.

37. Professor John Milne trained as a mining engineer and in 1876 went to Japan as a consultant to the government. He spent about twenty years in Japan, marrying a Japanese wife, and making a study of earthquakes which resulted in safer buildings and led to his being decorated by the emperor. After returning to England, Milne and his wife came to live at Shide, near Newport (house in background), where he died in July 1913.

38. Launching the Atherfield lifeboat involved sliding it down a 3 in 1 drop on a series of sleepers fixed to the 75 feet high cliff. Once on the beach, the lifeboat was placed on greased timbers to get her to the water's edge. Although the station had a short life, opening in 1890 and closing in 1915, it saved 157 lives.

1920-1929 Holidays for Many

39, 40. The Royal Naval College was established in 1903 in the grounds of Osborne House. Amongst those who trained there were Prince Edward (later King Edward VIII), Prince Albert (later King George VI) and Louis (later Earl) Mountbatten. The lack of demand for cadets after the 1st World War led to the College closing in 1921, leaving only Dartmouth College to provide the Navy with its officers. The lower photograph shows cadets learning carpentry.

41. The first Women's Institute on the Island opened at Ningwood in 1919 and by 1921 they had established eleven institutes across the County. In that year the County Federation was formed and in the following year they held their first fête in the grounds of Carisbrooke Castle. The Ryde St. Johns W.I. equipped the stall shown.

42. The first President of the Women's Institute on the Island was Laura, Lady Simeon (centre foreground); pictured here in the grounds of Carisbrooke Castle. Lady Simeon also became the first County Chairman in 1921, an office she held until ill-health forced her to retire in the 1940s.

43. The Upper Grade Boys School, St. Johns Road, Ryde was opened in 1883 to provide a higher and broader form of education, with girls joining the school early in the century. Once a year both pupils and staff assembled to mark Empire Day, as seen in this 1923 photograph.

44. Coach trips in the 1920s became more comfortable when firms such as Moss's Tours of Sandown fitted pneumatic tyres to their charabancs. A local photographer recorded these trippers on a tour from Sandown to Alum Bay in June 1925.

45. East and West Cowes are linked by a chain ferry across the River Medina. Occasionally, it has run aground, caught by the rapidly falling tide. When this happened foot passengers were rowed across, as seen here at West Cowes in August 1925.

46. The Ashey Racecourse opened in 1882 for both flat and hurdle racing, and for steeplechasing. In May 1925 there was a two day meeting; the weather was fine and a large crowd attended. One of the advantages of the site was its close proximity to Ashey Railway Station, just visible in the background.

48. After the 1st World War memorials to the fallen were erected in most towns and villages. This one, in St. Thomas's Square, Newport, was built in 1922, and the photograph shows the annual Armistice Day service in 1926. During week days the Square was usually crowded with carriers' carts collecting various goods to be delivered all over the Island.

47. (*Opposite page*) In the 1920s Cowes High Street suffered several times from flooding, as this view from its junction with Carvel Lane towards the Fountain Hotel shows. The sign 'Your Tobacconist' belonged to the shop of John Airs. Olivers, the footwear retailer, should have sold out of rubber boots.

49. The Needles & Alum Bay Pier Co. went into liquidation in 1926 and attempts were made to dispose of the pier. It fell into a bad state of disrepair and during a gale in February 1928 a particularly strong gust of wind tore away the decking and the central portion fell into the sea. The pier was never rebuilt, although the shore end was used by small pleasure craft.

50, 51. (*Opposite page*) One of the largest landslides the Island has known occurred on 26 July 1928 at Windy Corner, Blackgang. Some 120,000 tons fell from the upper cliff and completely blocked the Niton to Chale road. Due to the unstable land the road was never cleared, and a new road was built inland.

52. Dodson & Campbell Ltd. started to operate motor buses on the Island in 1921, but is best remembered by the name it adopted a year later: the Vectis Bus Co. Based at Newport, the company gradually extended its routes to cover the whole Island, and this 26-seater bus is shown waiting at Blackgang on the Newport – Ventnor route.

53. A family in their car on the Parade at Cowes. During Cowes Week, and for the rest of August, the Parade would have been crowded with visitors watching the yacht racing and hoping for a glimpse of the rich and famous coming ashore.

54. For centuries the cattle market was held in St. James's Square, Newport, but by the mid-1920s the increase in traffic and concerns about hygiene lead to it being moved. Newport Borough Council obtained a site in South Street and in 1928 opened a new enclosed market at a cost of £8,000, which provided both the livestock and marketeers with cover.

55. In the 1920s concert parties were popular with visitors and 'The Gaieties' are a good example of a London group performing at the Vectis Hall on the Esplanade, Sandown. The entertainment was described as 'brilliant, bright and breezy, without a trace of anything distasteful'.

56. St. Lawrence Hall, Ventnor, became the retirement home of Admiral of the Fleet, Earl Jellicoe, which is where this photograph was taken in 1929 with his son, Viscount Brocas, and one of his daughters. The Admiral, famous for his action at the Battle of Jutland in 1916, had retired from the navy in 1924 and was created an earl the following year.

1930-1939 The Hopeful Thirties

57. Chillerton School held a traditional May Day festival in 1931. There was a programme of maypole and country dancing, plus singing and acting. The queen, Joan Salter, led her two trainbearers around the playground. The collection amounting to £1-5-7½d (approx. £1.28) was for the summer outing.

58. (*Following pages*) This aerial photograph of the River Medina looking towards West Cowes proves the popularity of steam yachts well into the 1930s. In the centre, standing alone, is the church of St. Faith, built in 1909. Centre right is the local gas works with its riverside coaling wharf.

59. The dilapidated eighteenth century Newtown Town Hall was presented to the National Trust in 1932. In the following year repairs, by the Cowes builders H.E. Day & Sons, were able to begin due to the generosity of a secret society, 'The Ferguson Gang', an anonymous philanthropic group concerned about the loss of historic buildings in the 1920s and 30s. Its first use after restoration was as a youth hostel.

60. A fine summer's day at Sandown in 1934 with two ladies enjoying a walk along the footpath adjoining Culver Parade. In the background, on the beach, are the bathing tents which had earlier in the century replaced the bathing machines. Most seaside towns had street photographers who photographed passing visitors on the chance of custom, and this is an example of their work.

61. During the 1930s large quantities of chalk were extracted from Pan Pit near Newport and taken by train to the Cement Mills on the west bank of the River Medina. The 'Terrier' engine No. 8 *Freshwater* was built in 1876. It arrived on the Island in 1913 and is shown propelling empty trucks through Newport to Pan Pit. The *Freshwater* has since been restored and is today used on the Isle of Wight Railway at Havenstreet.

62. The first six double-decker buses purchased by the local bus company, Southern Vectis, were landed from barges at Yarmouth in 1937, and here one of them is shown standing in St. James's Square, Newport, soon after its arrival.

63. After the Isle of Wight became a county in 1890 its offices were on several sites in Newport. In 1936 it was decided to demolish the Swan Hotel in the High Street and build a County Hall. The new building was opened in October 1938 by Lord Bayford, President of the County Councils Association.

64. The arrival of the five day working week and the great expansion in leisure time that resulted lead to this open-air swimming pool and café being opened at Lakeside, Wootton Bridge, in August 1938. It was designed by the Shanklin architects, Harrison & Gilkes and was a good example of contemporary architecture. Sadly, it fell into disuse after the 1970s and was later demolished.

65. Every May a special Spring Market was held in the Newport Cattle Market, and here the auctioneer David Dockrill is disposing of sheep at the 1938 market. William Hurst & Son is an old established firm which is still in business today.

66. Until May 1938 lorries and cars were brought across from Lymington to Yarmouth on open barges which were towed behind the passenger ferry or by the tug *Jumsev*, as in this photograph at Yarmouth slipway. In May 1938 the new double-ended ferry *Lymington* came into service.

67. For at least 200 years ship's pilots have been guiding vessels into Portsmouth and Southampton. The Trinity House Pilot Vessel *Bembridge* was stationed at the eastern entrance to the Solent, from where pilots were taken by a launch to board incoming shipping.

68. The new Bembridge lifeboat *Jesse Lumb* was built by J. S. White at Cowes in 1939 and was launched by Miss A. Lumb in memory of her brother. The new boat was the second motor lifeboat at Bembridge and was on station until 1970, and during her service was launched 294 times and saved 280 lives.

69. The lodge to Northwood House, Cowes, was designed by John Nash and built in the early nineteenth century. In the 1920s the house and ground passed to the local council who in 1939 had the lodge demolished to make way for municipal baths.

70. By 1937 the impending threat of war persuaded the government to build a chain of radar stations along the east and south coasts of England. St. Boniface Down, Ventnor, was the most westerly site. Three 240ft wooden receiver masts were erected by October 1938 (left), followed in 1939, by three 365ft steel towers. In August 1940 the station was put out of action by German bombers, but fortunately only one person was injured. The station was back on the air by the following November.

1940-1949 War and Peace

71. During the 2nd World War men and women from all branches of the services were posted to the Isle of Wight. The 6th Battalion of the 6th Black Watch arrived in June 1940 when the threat of invasion was at its height, and can here be seen training in a farmyard at Havenstreet. In the foreground the soldiers are practicing with machine guns.

72. By 1940 a quarter of the Southern Vectis Bus Co. staff had joined the forces. Only three conductors were left, so the Company recruited conductresses to make up the numbers, one of whom is seen here in her summer issue white coat. Note the shrouded headlight of the bus.

73. In May 1940 the Government broadcast an appeal for men to enlist in the Local Defence Volunteer Corp. It was renamed the Home Guard two months later. No. 4 Platoon Newport Home Guard, 'D' Company, West Wight Battalion, consisted mainly of Southern Vectis staff, who are seen here with one of their buses.

74. The remains of a German Junkers JU87b outside the St. Lawrence Hotel, near Ventnor in August 1940. It was shot down by a Hurricane whilst attacking a convoy in the Channel, and was the first German aircraft to crash in the Isle of Wight.

75. On the night of 4/5 May, 1942 the residents of East and West Cowes had good reason to be thankful for the presence of the Polish destroyer *Blyskawica* at J.S. White's shipyard. The anti-aircraft barrage she kept up all night did much to prevent German bombers totally devastating the town. At one time the destroyer had to have her ammunition stocks replenished by boat from Portsmouth.

76. Shortages during the 2nd World War lead to metal being recycled for armaments and paper being pulped to provide newspapers and books. Ryde's Guides and Scouts organised a waste paper collection and standing on this pile of books in St. Thomas's Square, Ryde, are Maureen Barton and Spencer Billett.

77. This was the result of a daylight hit and run air attack on Shanklin in January 1943 in which 23 people were killed. The Roman Catholic Church and Landguard Road Fire Station were destroyed. Three of the firemen killed had just returned from a period of duty in the London Blitz.

78. Hazelwood House, Ryde, was built in the nineteenth century and used for many years by the Y.M.C.A. During the 2nd World War it was occupied by the Royal Marines, four of whom were killed when German fighter-bombers straffed the town and Hazelwood was badly damaged.

79. With more land under cultivation and many farm workers in the forces, women from all walks of life were encouraged to join the Land Army. Here two are shown looking after the cart horses at Rossiters, Wellow.

80. Having gained supremacy in the air over England by the end of 1943, the Allied forces started to prepare for 'Operation Overlord'. In the weeks leading up to D-Day on 5/6 June 1944 the Isle of Wight was crammed with troops. Here the 1st Independent Guards are rehearsing the landings ahead in Thorness Bay whilst waiting to be shipped to France.

81. (*Opposite page*) Like millions all over Britain, children and mums of Lower Bellevue Road, Cowes, celebrated the end of the war in Europe with a VE Day street party. Although food was still rationed, everybody found something for the children to enjoy. Note the street air-raid shelter in the background.

82. After being away for six years as a troop ship, the liner *Queen Mary* returned to her home port of Southampton in August 1945. Early the following year she made six voyages to New York carrying 9,000 G.I. Brides and their 4,000 children. The photograph shows the 81,000 ton liner passing Ryde in 1946; still wearing its grey war-time livery.

83. In the 1930s the Isle of Wight Dairies Ltd introduced Shetland ponies to pull their milk carts around Ryde. This photograph was taken outside their depot in West Street shortly after the war. In the 1950s they were replaced by electric floats, but many milkmen mourned their departure as the ponies were so familiar with their routes they required little attention, leaving the milkmen free to make the deliveries on their rounds.

1950-1959 The New Elizabethan Age

84. Seaview had the only suspension pier on the Island. The 1,000 feet long pier was designed by a local man, Frank Caws, and modelled on the famous Brighton Chain Pier. It was opened in 1881 and ferries en route from Portsmouth to Bembridge called in there. Due to wartime service when troops were stationed on the pier it fell into a bad state of repair, and it was finally destroyed by a storm in December 1950.

85. The maiden flight of the Princess flying boat was on 22 August 1952, when it took 35 minutes to circle the Isle of Wight. Designed to carry 200 passengers, this huge flying boat was built by Saunders-Roe at East Cowes. Unfortunately the project was dropped due to development problems with the engines and the aircraft was scrapped in 1967.

86. In 1951 the new ferry *Shanklin* came into service, joining her two sister ships on the Portsmouth-Ryde route. Each carried over 1,300 passengers. The need for all three ferries is well-illustrated in this photograph of holidaymakers on Ryde Pier waiting to return to the mainland, taken on a typical August Saturday in 1952.

87. (*Following pages*) With the coronation of the Queen in June 1953, austere post-war Britain took the opportunity to relax and enjoy itself. This arch across St. James's Square, Newport is an example of how Islanders celebrated, together with street parties and gathering round primitive flickering television sets to watch the first coronation to be televised.

88. Heavy snow falls and hard frosts were experienced across Hampshire and the Isle of Wight in January 1954, and Wootton Bridge did not escape. The main road has been cleared, but the snow is still thick outside the Tide Mill and the 'Sloop Inn'.

89. A leading motor car and tractor engineers was Fowlers (Isle of Wight) Ltd of the High Street and Pyle Street, Newport, seen here exhibiting at the annual County Agricultural Show.

90. This photograph shows the fourth Ventnor Pier. The first was built in 1863, and the last (this one) was formerly opened in 1955. The new pier which was designed by a local architect Basil L. Pheleps, was 683 feet long and the pavilion could accommodate 500. By the 1990s it needed £800,000 to be spent on its repair, and so was demolished in 1992/93.

91. The Italian steamer *Iano* sheltered from a storm in Sandown Bay in November 1957. Her anchors slipped and she was driven broadside onto the beach. Four of the crew stayed on board whilst the remainder were taken ashore. A bulldozer removed a large quantity of sand and shingle, which enabled the ship to be refloated some days later.

92. The ferry *Carisbrooke Castle* was built in Southampton by J.I.Thornycroft & Co Ltd., entering service in May 1959. The once familiar *Carisbrooke Castle* was Red Funnel's first purpose designed passenger/vehicle ferry, and was capable of carrying 45 cars on the main deck. The ferry was withdrawn in 1974 and sold to an Italian company.

93. In the early 1950s Christopher Cockerell owned a Norfolk boatyard, and it was there that he began experimenting with the reduction of friction between a boat's hull and the water. By using a can of cat food inside a coffee tin and reversed air-flow from a vacuum cleaner, he proved his theory that a craft could be supported on a cushion of air. He then produced a working model which was shown to the Government. After much delay, they awarded the contract to build the first manned hovercraft to Saunders-Roe of East Cowes, and on 11 June 1959 the SRN1 was shown to the world. Sir Christopher died in June 1999.

94. The 1950s have been described as the halcyon days for Ryde Carnival, which was originally founded in 1888. The Southern Electricity Board annually entered a float and are here shown portraying the famous donkey in the wheel at Carisbrooke Castle.

95. A new way of bringing cars to the Island was introduced in the 1950s when Silver City Airways started a service from Southampton to Bembridge Airport. A twin-engine 'Bristol 170' could carry several cars with a journey time of nine minutes. This aircraft appears to need assistance to get out of the mud.

1960-1969 The Expanding Sixties

96. One man who brought the Isle of Wight to the nation's notice was Newport milkman Terry Perkins, better known in the pop world as Craig Douglas. He sold over five million records and is here photographed on his return to the Island in 1960 for two sell-out concerts, joined by Newport Carnival Queen, Janice Hall.

97. The October of 1960 was the wettest on record, and severe flooding early in the month virtually cut off Newport from the rest of the Island. Here in Carisbrooke Road the depth of water brought the traffic to a halt.

98. A railway bridge on the Newport-Sandown line was first built over the road at Coppins Bridge, Newport, in 1879. It was replaced in 1920 by the bridge in the photograph, which itself was dismantled in 1960, four years after the line had closed.

99. Records of the tide mill at Wootton Bridge extend back to the thirteenth century, when it was owned by Quarr Abbey. Being ideally situated on Wootton Creek, it was accessible by road and water. This photograph, taken shortly before it was demolished in 1963, shows the hatches used for loading and unloading from vessels.

100. (*Opposite page*) In the early years of the twentieth century the Island's railway system gradually extended to a total of 55½ miles of track, serving 33 stations and halts. The 1950s and 1960s saw the system gradually shrink, until in 1967 under 13 miles of track remained, and only 8 stations. This photograph, taken at Newport a few years before closure in 1966, shows a train leaving for Cowes.

101. The Queen and the Duke of Edinburgh came to the Island on a formal two day visit in July 1965, on the first of which the Queen installed Earl Mountbatten as Governor of the Isle of Wight at Carisbooke Castle. They are seen here arriving at the Castle, announced by a trumpet fanfare and a royal salute.

102. (*Opposite page, top*) By 1965 Christopher Cockerell's hovercraft had been developed sufficiently to enable Hovertravel Ltd. to be formed to charter an SRN6 to operate a permanent hovercraft service between Ryde and the mainland. Today two modern 98-seater hovercraft cover the four miles between Ryde and Southsea in 10 minutes.

103. (*Opposite page, bottom*) Britten-Norman Ltd. was formed in 1953 to convert aircraft for crop spraying, and then, in the late 1950s, the development of the hovercraft. In 1963 the company turned its attention to designing and producing an entirely new aircraft, 'The Islander', at its Bembridge factory. The prototype G-ATCT first flew from Bembridge Airport in June 1965. It was a success from the outset, particularly for short haul passenger and freight routes. To date (August 1999) about 1,000 have been built.

104. The *Queen Mary* was undoubtedly one of the most popular liners ever built. She was in service from 1936 until 1967, when on the morning of 31 October she left Southampton for the last time. Here we see her from Cowes Parade, having rounded the Brambles on her 13,000 mile journey to Long Beach, California, where she is now a floating tourist centre and hotel.

105. The X design of yachts was created on the Island by the designer Alfred Westmacott in 1909. It became a very popular class and is the oldest design of keel boat still racing. In 1967, 141 boats of the X class raced at Cowes. In the background is the guardship, the cruiser *H.M.S. Tiger* which was first commissioned in 1959.

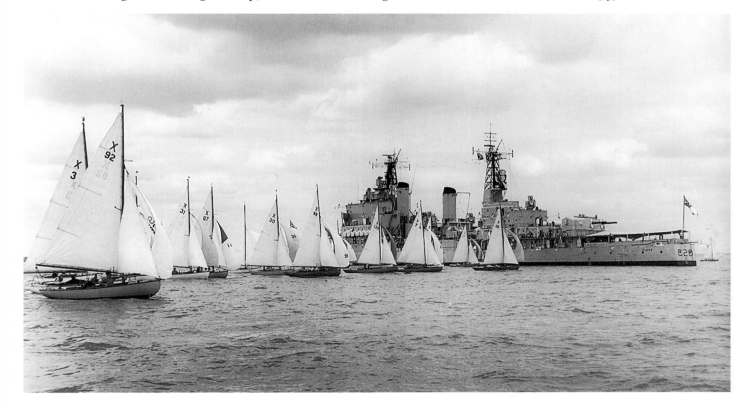

106. In April 1966 the railway line from Shanklin to Ventnor was closed. Soon afterwards contractors started to take up the line – this was at Wroxall, the only intermediate station. Today the area is mainly covered by a car park and houses, but the bridge survives.

107. Ryde Pier Tramway was opened in 1864 with horse-drawn trams. By 1871 it had been extended to St. John's Road Station, but in 1880 was reduced to only the length of the Pier. The petrol-engine cars in this photograph arrived in 1927 and were later fitted with diesel engines. The tramway was closed in January 1969.

108. The work load placed on County Councils after the 2nd World War called for much more office space. Plans for a large extension to County Hall were approved and in 1967 work started to demolish all the properties between County Hall and Sea Street, during which seven brick and stone-lined wells were found.

109. In 1966 a contract was placed by the Government with Saunders-Roe for a three stage launch rocket. It was named 'Black Arrow' and was statically tested at the High Down Rocket Test Site, above the Needles in 1967. Later it went on to Woomera, South Australia for launching.

1970-1979 The Changing Seventies

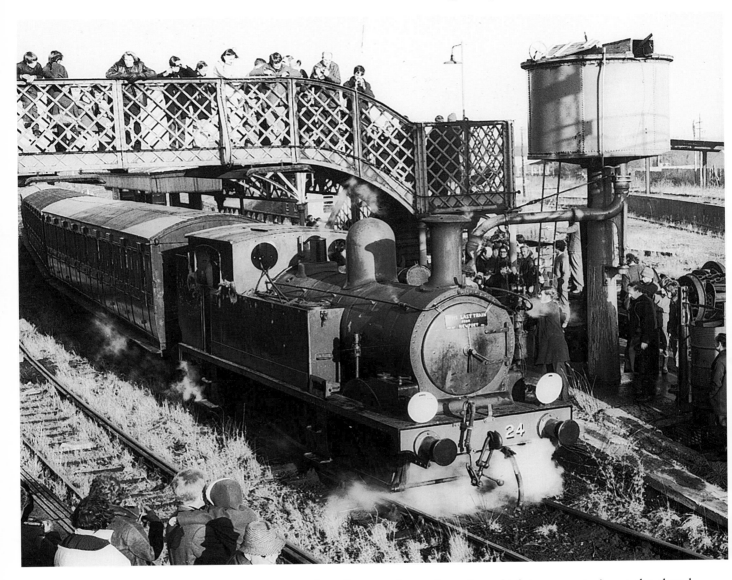

110. The Wight Locomotive Society owned a railway engine and coaches which it was restoring at the closed Newport Station. On 24 January 1971 they had to move to a new home at Havenstreet. The engine, No. 24, is seen here leaving Newport with the coaches for the new site. This was the last day that steam trains were seen at Newport.

111. The years 1973 and 1974 saw big changes in the Newport Harbour area. The old railway viaduct and the bridge across the river were demolished. This was part of a large scheme to make land available to build the Newport Relief Road, now named Medina Way.

112. The town of Ryde became a borough by Royal Charter in 1868 and carried out several schemes to make the area more attractive to both residents and visitors. In accordance with the Local Government Act of 1974 Ryde became part of the new Medina Borough, and pictured here are the last Mayor, Raymond Bourn, and his fellow councillors and chief officers.

113. Stephen (Steve to everybody) Ross, a local estate agent, entered politics in 1967, when he became a county councillor. In 1974 he contested the Island parliamentary seat and became the first Liberal M.P. for more than 50 years, overturning a Conservative majority of more than 17,000 to win the seat by nearly 8,000 votes. After his retirement in 1987 he was created Baron Ross of Newport.

114. The local bus company purchased a number of new 'Bristol' double-deckers in the 1950s, and in 1973 to 1975, five were converted to open-top, so that passengers could enjoy, in fine weather, some of the Island's scenic routes. Here a bus load of visitors is passing through Shanklin on its way to Ventnor.

115. A chain ferry has been operating across the River Medina between East and West Cowes since 1859. It stayed in private hands until 1901 when it was purchased by Cowes Council. In 1974 the Isle of Wight County Council awarded Fairy Marine of East Cowes the contract to build the present ferry. It cost £280,000, and was launched in January 1976.

116. The *M.V. Netley Castle* was the first Red Funnel ferry since 1931 not to have been built at Southampton by J.I Thornycroft Co Ltd. She entered service in June 1974 as the company's first purpose built double-ended car ferry. In the next year she cruised around the Silver Jubilee Fleet Review.

117. The third Island Pop Festival in August 1970 at Afton, starring the American singer-songwriter Bob Dylan, lasted for five days and attracted over 200,000 fans. Together with the holiday makers, this brought the total to over half a million visitors that week. The Afton arena covered 20 acres and after the event there were mile-long bus queues with 5,000 leaving the Island each hour.

118. In October 1970 the Island nearly suffered a catastrophic ecological disaster. As the result of a collision, followed by a large explosion, in which 13 members of the crew were killed, the burning tanker *Pacific Glory*, began drifting towards Sandown Bay. An extensive sea rescue operation was mounted to stem the flow of 70,000 gallons of oil into the sea. After a long battle the oil was pumped out into smaller tankers and the Island beaches were saved.

119. In June 1977 thousands of Islanders crowded onto Ryde Pier to watch the Review of the Fleet during the Queen's Silver Jubilee celebrations. At the top can be seen some of the warships. On the right is the Royal Yacht *Britannia*, with the Queen on board, passing down the lines, led by the Trinity House vessel *Patricia* (top left).

120. The Island's municipal lottery was launched in 1976, with the three local authorities hoping for good annual profits. In December 1978 Mrs Christine Ellis won the lottery prize and is seen here at Lane End Stationers, Bembridge receiving her £1,000 cheque from Douglas Naylor.

121. The Prince of Wales made his first official visit to the Island in June 1982. He came to name the £3 million Mountbatten Centre, near Newport, after his great uncle. The Prince is pictured on the same day in St. James's Square, Newport, before unveiling a bust of Earl Mountbatten.

122. A local man, John Ackroyd, designed the 'Thrust 2' car, which was built in one of the boat sheds at Ranalagh Works, Fishbourne, between 1979 and 1981. This photograph shows her being loaded on the ferry at East Cowes. In October 1993 'Thrust 2', driven by Richard Noble, gained the World Land Speed Record, at a speed of 633 m.p.h.

123. The *St. Catherine* was the first of the new super car ferries and is seen here going astern out of Fishbourne. She was launched in March 1983 and entered service in July. For the first time passengers were asked to leave their cars and enjoy the ample accommodation above.

124. The Princess of Wales flew into Ryde by helicopter in May 1985. In glorious sunshine, attended by the Lord Lieutenant, Sir John Nicholson, her first visit was to Adelaide Court residential home and the adjoining club. The Princess went on to visit a training centre for the young, then to a Business Centre in Sandown, where large crowds waited to greet her.

125. The first convict fleet to depart for Australia sailed from the Mother Bank off Ryde on the 13 May 1787. To mark the 200th anniversary an exhibition was mounted in St. Thomas Heritage Centre, Ryde. It was opened by the Queen, who was accompanied by the Duke of Edinburgh.

126. The infamous hurricane which struck the South of England in October 1987 badly damaged Shanklin Pier. It had been built between 1888 and 1890, surviving many storms, but the hurricane carried away the whole centre section, including the theatre. Next day sightseers saw tons of debris on the beach. Elsewhere on the island, hundreds of trees were destroyed and many buildings badly damaged.

127. By the 1980s the old Yarmouth bridge was in need of replacing. It had been in use since 1860, and could no longer handle the demands of modern traffic. The County Council had a new bridge built, with a centre opening span, at a cost of £2.4 million. It was opened in September 1987 by the former local M.P., Lord Ross.

128. The donkeys at Carisbrooke Castle have been popular with the public for the last 200 years. They are used to tread the wheel which raises and lowers the bucket in the Castle's well. In May 1988 the donkey Jessica gave birth to the first foal to have been born in the Castle for many years. It was named Elizabeth to commemorate the 400th anniversary of the Armada.

129. Carisbrooke Castle was built in the early years of the millennium and remains one of the Island's most enduring landmarks. Although it has long since ceased to be a fortress, it is used and enjoyed by residents and visitors. These days 'living history' events add both colour and meaning and, as in July 1988, are often supported by local schools.

130. Since the 1970s local radio has become a popular part of Island life. B.B.C. Radio Solent is pictured here broadcasting from a country fair in the grounds of Osborne House in August 1989. We also now have our even more local 'Isle of Wight Radio'.

131. Steam trains ceased on the Ryde to Shanklin line in 1967, to be replaced by electric trains which had been built between 1924 and 1935 for the London Underground (foreground). They in turn were later replaced in 1987 by completely refurbished second-hand Underground stock built in 1938 (middle).

132. A National School was first built on this site in Newport in 1816, but was rebuilt in 1909 from the designs of a local architect, Percy Stone, at a cost of £5,000. The new buildings, which could take over 600 children, were opened by Princess Beatrice in October 1909. The school closed at the end of 1989, when pupils moved to a new site at Carisbrooke.

1990-1999 Towards the New Millennium

133. Because of the difficulties in achieving administrative separation from Hampshire, the Isle of Wight County Council began its life in April 1890, one year later than similar authorities elsewhere. On 3 April 1990 the Councillors, led by their Chairman, Bernard Pratt, attended a centenary service in Newport, and afterwards this photograph was taken on the steps of County Hall.

134. (*Opposite page*) The first hospital to be built on the Island was at Ryde in 1848 and for the next 140 years it was enlarged and modernised, and remained the County Hospital. In the late 1980s it was decided to centralise the health services which resulted in the building of a new hospital on a site adjacent to the small St. Mary's Hospital at Newport. The new and somewhat controversial St. Mary's Hospital was formally opened on Monday 23 September 1991 by H.R.H. Princess Alexandra.

135. The years 1990-91 saw the biggest development on Ryde Esplanade since the last century. Upon recently reclaimed land an ice skating rink with leisure facilities was built, together with a large car park. The project was completed and opened in the spring of 1991. To the east a yachting harbour was created and this was finished in time for the Ryde Regatta in July.

136. 'Red Funnel' took delivery of the *Balmoral* in 1949 and for the next 19 years she worked the Cowes to Southampton ferry service. In 1968 she was taken by P. & H. Campbell Ltd. for Bristol Channel excursions. Then Waverley Excursions Ltd. obtained her in 1985, and has since done many excursions around Britain's shores. In June 1992 she made a special trip up the River Medina and is seen here turning in Newport Harbour.

137. In 1993 it was the turn of the Isle of Wight to host the 5th Island Games. The bowling green at Carisbrooke Castle was the site for the opening ceremony on 3 July. It was performed in fine sunny weather in the presence of the Princess Royal. The Isle of Wight team is marching past the dais.

138. As a result of houses destroyed during the 2nd World War there was an urgent need for replacements in 1945. One of the quick answers was the erection of these Acon prefabricated bungalows at Seaview Road, Cowes. Although they were only supposed to last ten years, they proved popular and some were occupied until the end of 1994, when they were replaced by brick-built houses.

139. Lord Mottistone served in the 2nd World War as a naval commander escorting convoys in the Atlantic and Mediterranean. He succeeded to his title in 1966 and retired as a Captain in the following year. He was appointed Lord Lieutenant of the County in 1986, taking an active interest in a wide range of Island matters. The Queen installed Lord Mottistone as Governor in 1992, and he retired from both offices in December 1995.

140. With the idea of raising the profile of the Island and to generate funds for charities, the local council started to issue Isle of Wight Ecus in sets of four costing £3.95 in April 1996. However, the Council had breached the Coinage Act, but when sales ceased in the September, 8,500 tokens had been sold.

141. The full size replica sailing vessel *Matthew* called at Cowes in April 1996 bound for the International Festival of the Sea at Bristol. From there in 1997 she crossed the Atlantic, with a crew of 19, to commemorate the 500th anniversary of John Cabot's crossing.

142. A familiar site at Cowes Week for many years was the Royal Yacht *Britannia*. The public enjoyed watching the Duke of Edinburgh and other Royals coming and going. On 22 November 1997 she entered Portsmouth Harbour flying her long paying-off pennant and was decommissioned. She is now on exhibition in Scotland.

143. Agriculture is still an important industry on the Island, although farming methods have changed radically during the last 80 years. The first tractors were introduced after the 1st World War, but they did not have much impact until the 1940s. Today large tractors plough six or more furrows at a time across large fields. Unfortunately miles of hedgerows have been lost to accommodate these huge machines, but the Island still has some 10,000 hectares (24,710 acres) under cultivation, with wheat and barley remaining the principal crops.

144. The organisers of the 100th County Agricultural Show in July 1998 were pleased to be able to exhibit 'Thrust SSC', the fastest car in the World. After the success of 'Thrust 2', Richard Noble decided to aim for the ultimate Land Speed Record - the first car to break the sound barrier. With that aim he directed the building of 'Thrust SCC' which on 15 October 1996 became the first supersonic car at 763 miles per hour.

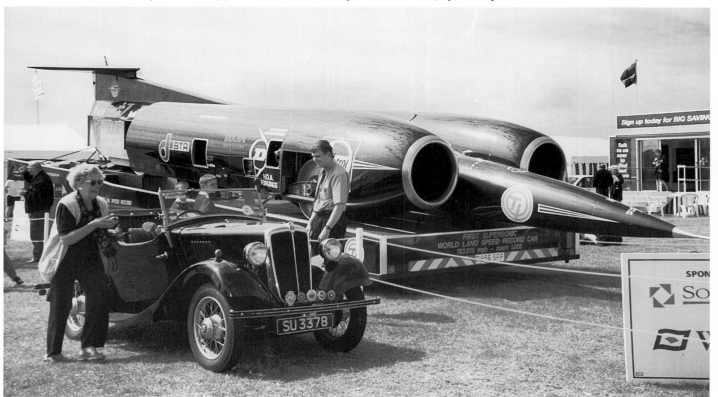

145. In 1991 Red Funnel brought into their Hi-Speed Service, 'Red Jet 1' and 'Red Jet 2'. Each carried 138 passengers on the 22 minute journey and they soon became popular. To meet public demand a third vessel was built at F.B.M. at Cowes. 'Red Jet 3' is slightly larger, carrying 190 passengers and started operating in July 1998.

146. A vessel in which Islanders always take a great interest is Cunard's *Queen Elizabeth 2*. She was launched in 1967 by the Queen, and made her maiden voyage two years later from her home port, Southampton. Whenever the 'Q.E. 2' is in the Solent she attracts attention and is watched and photographed from Ryde Pier Head and other vantage points.

147. After a wait of many years the Island now has a Sainsbury's. At a cost of £15 million, the brilliant white clad supermarket was opened in April 1999 at Hunnyhill, Newport. The area was landscaped and a new road, Hunny Cross Way, was built to provide access to the petrol filling station. The design of the store is new and will take Island shopping into the new millennium.